MW01610152

12
Blssoms

by

Jo P. Lo and Mike Stolt

illustrated by Claire LaRose

DEAR KEITH,

PLEASURE TO ME YOU MY NEW FRIEND.

GOD BLESS,

Jo P. Lo

Days drift by like dandelion seeds in the breeze.

But it's with the satisfaction of an old gardener with leathery, thorn-scarred hands and

a sunburst of wrinkles around his eyes,

that we gaze with the sun at our backs

upon the flowers of our lives.

Some we remember planting,

some appear as wonderful weeds.

A handful of beautiful truths,

a brace of blossoms so brilliant

that we gather a bouquet

and rush to give it away as fast as possible.

1

COMPASSION

Give the guy a break.

Give yourself a break.

2
HUMILITY

The absence of self-assertion.

The absence of pride.

Humility is the hallmark of
an enlightened person.

3

CAPACITY TO LOVE IS LIMITED BY DEPTH OF PERCEPTION

A child does not love an adult with
the same depth
as an adult loves a child.

Likewise, an adult's ability to love
differs from person to person,
just as their perception
of the world differs.

Embrace this truth
or live, and love, in frustration.

4
BE ENTHUSIASTIC

Muster the energy
to attack each day
with a burst of promise.

It's becoming, exciting,
winning and contagious.

It will get you
married, hired, elected
and happy.

5
ENGAGE

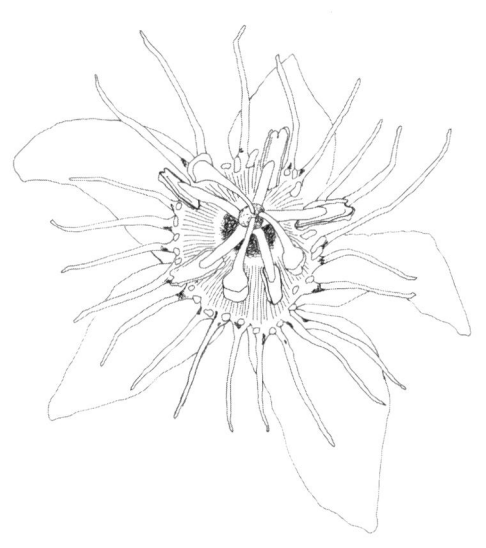

The timing is never right for the things that matter in life.

Don't let fear, laziness, or a lack of confidence hold you back...

...from having kids,
birthing a business,
or righting wrongs.

6

GRAPPLE

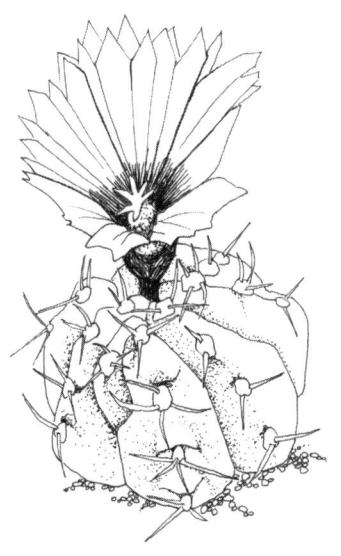

Two men in a fight,
a real fight,
will end up fighting alone
in a corner ~
desperate, exhausted, scared.

All of your life's jugular decisions
will be made
in this position.

Learn to like it.

7

YOUR MIND IS NOT YOUR FRIEND

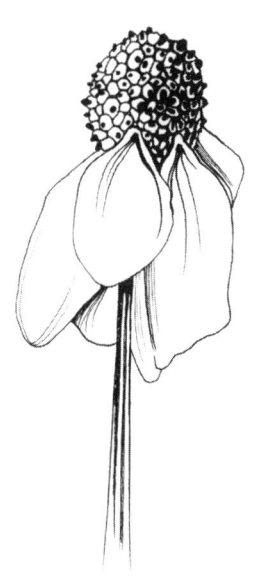

Your mind dominates you,
fights you,
toys with you.

Left untamed,
it will conquer
a weak body and soul.

8

INTEGRITY

If you are perfect in every way
except that you cannot be trusted
to do what you say you will do,

you are flawed
through and through.

"I'll call you sometime and we'll have lunch," you say .

You'd better soon have lunch.

9
ASK FOR HELP

It is the beginning of the end when you think to yourself,

"I think I've got all this figured out."

10

LOVE THE
MUNDANE

Life is not an
endless celebration
of successes.

Life is mowing grass,
building fences,
washing dishes.

Work that stresses your back
frees your mind.

Mindless tasks are the soils
in which brilliance blooms.

11
DAILY
ARRANGEMENT

We drink deep the toxic gruel
that is our daily grind.

We sleep little,
work much, and
steal time from family.

Balance.

Meditate.
Bond with those you love.
Exercise your body and mind.

Make the most of
the scraps of time.

Sweeten your day with
life's intangibles,
life's immeasurables,
life's unscoreables...

... thousand-mile stares,
stretching,
holding doors for strangers.

12
FINISH WHAT YOU START

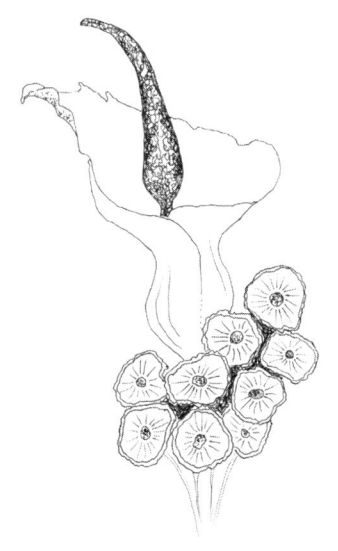

The key to success in life is
the follow through.

The most brilliant beginnings...

a business idea
a golf swing
a relationship
a punch
a job

...are meaningless
unless you follow through.

Quitting can become a nasty habit.

Finish.

Finish Strong.

ACKNOWLEDGMENTS

Thanks Mike Stolt. You are a writer and have been a super partner on this book.

Thanks Claire LaRose. You are an artist and a wonderful one at that.

Thanks Marty Morris. You have been a selfless advisor throughout this whole process.

Thanks Bill Rogers. You were a stranger who became a friend inside of 90 seconds and guided me through a mine field.

Thanks Tim Leonhart. For your business guidance via Book Masters Inc.

Thanks Kelli Gustafson. Your skill, patience, and advice were appreciated for the cover and graphics.

Jo P. Lo